MINDFULNESS
& MEDITATION

BEGINNERS GUIDE TO RAISING YOUR
VIBRATION, ATTRACTING ABUNDANCE
AND FINDING INNER PEACE

DISCLAIMER

Introduction

'What is now proved was once only imagined.' – William Blake

We are used to leading life at a very frantic pace. Our uncertainty about the future makes us worried and our endless responsibilities and deadlines can seem overwhelming. Demands on our mind and body are ceaseless from the professional as well as personal fronts and the results are evident on all of us. Fast paced lifestyles arising from demanding deadlines coupled with the percolation of technology into personal space have left us burn out and unnerved. If we continue on like this, fatigue sets in and overwhelms the mind and body leaving behind a drained out individual continuing on like a soulless robot. We need to get out of this cycle and reclaim our lives to enjoy peaceful and satisfying times while we inhabit the planet. We all deserve more than just a passing glimpse of a peaceful and tranquil moment. Moreover a serene mind and a calm body are more likely to succeed in all areas of our lives than stressed and burn out souls. Meditation can bring us to a place of inner peace and tranquility.

All of this stimulation and the pressures to multi-task make it hard for us to focus on anything for too long. Thoughts come and go constantly, sometimes forgotten and other times added to the already long to-do list. We tend to forget to take care of ourselves as we rush through the day, just hoping to get as much done as possible. Meditation can help us to slow down, release stress, and do better in our lives than ever before. Living in a cluttered, chaotic home can be very difficult and stressful, but a cluttered and hectic mind is carried with us throughout the day and is much more damaging to our goals and to accomplish what we want. Mindfulness goes hand in hand with meditation to help us focus our minds and handle stress with ease. Mindfulness is also key to manifesting abundance as it brings us to a place of higher awareness from where we can observe our thoughts and in turn let go of any negativity that does not serve us.

The beauty of mindfulness and meditation is that they are quite simple, and yet yield major benefits in our daily lives. While most people just muddle through their days confused, stressed, and unable to easily see options in difficult situations; those who practice these methods teach their minds and bodies to stay calm in the face of stressful situations, think clearly, and are able to reduce or even remove the fight or flight reflex. Even when there is no stress or pressure upon us, our ability to think clearly, focus attention, and control our thoughts to avoid wandering are strengthened through meditation and mindfulness practice. These are not just new-age religion or Eastern religious practices; they are tools that everyone can learn to make better decisions, gain deeper insight and knowledge, and even improve the brain's communication within itself. They open doors to creativity and imagination while also keeping us grounded in reality and in each moment of our lives. These two powerful tools can change your life by bringing you to a place of higher vibration from where you can manifest your dreams and live joyfully and in peace.

Table of Contents

Chapter 1

Guide to Meditation and Mindfulness

Meditation, when practiced with regularity and discipline, can transform one's life. It's easy to see how meditation and mindfulness can provide a real benefit to our lives, but to actually understand how amazing these methods can make you feel, you must commit to making them a part of your daily life. They can't be done only a few times here and there, for best results you must practice each and every day. The beauty is that you can find the time when it works best for you. Some people prefer to meditate in the early hours of the morning when the sun is coming up; others prefer to practice in the evening right before going to sleep. Regardless when you choose to practice, makes sure you will be undisturbed.

Initially, it may seem that you are wasting time that you could be putting to good use doing something more important, however as you commit daily you will see the benefits of your practice. You will feel more comfortable with yourself and who you are, make better decisions, be able to concentrate on the important tasks before you, and even fall asleep faster. These benefits alone will be the proof that your time has been well invested, not wasted.

Benefits of Meditation

Meditation has many benefits for both the mind and the body. Meditation is more than just a technique of relaxation; it helps to condition the brain so that it actually functions more effectively and communicates well from one area of the brain to another. Your mind becomes much more open for creativity, allowing you to use your creativeness and imagination easily. This does not mean that only people who require creativity to create art, music, or writings should meditate; creativity can help you to think outside the box, improve decision making skills by helping you to see more options, and even help you to see possible outcomes of decisions that you planning on making.

Meditation also helps in understanding ourselves, our feelings, and why we react in certain unwanted ways. We have been conditioned to react and think in certain ways based on our up bringing, the culture in which we were raised and what we observed socially and from the media. Meditation will bring you to a place of higher understanding of yourself and help you understand why you operate the way you do. You can learn to stop and quickly calm yourself when unwanted feelings arise, analyze your feelings or even put them on hold if necessary. Meditation also improves your ability to think more logically and cultivates a person in you that searches for peaceful understanding, strives for greater awareness and is in touch with Higher Self. It helps you to communicate with others and express yourself clearly and effectively. It also allows you to become more patient, with yourself and with others.

As a benefit of improved brain function, performance at work as well as academically improves as you improve your memory, focus your attention more effectively, and effortlessly communicate thoughts and ideas. You become more confident in your abilities, which are automatically reinforced because there is much less doubt in yourself. Physical benefits of mediation include decreased blood pressure, less frequent and intense headaches, improved pain management and much more.

One of the most important benefits of meditation is improved sleep. With less stress and the ability to let go of your negative thoughts and worries it is much easier to fall asleep and allow your mind to work as your body rests. Restful sleep is very important for brain function, but many people do not realize that sleep can keep our bodies healthy and help us cope with the physical stress of illness as well. The physical benefit of reduced stress and restful sleep is tied to normal levels of cortisol. The more stressed we feel, the more cortisol is released in our system. Cortisol is that nasty hormone that makes it easy for us to gain fat, especially around the belly, and so one could say that it becomes easier to lose or maintain weight with daily meditation practice.

Benefits of Mindfulness

Mindfulness is different from meditation in that it is related more to focusing attention and living in the present moment. Mindfulness is the state of being grounded and focusing your attention on the external environment, being aware of your surroundings, colors, textures, smells and sounds. Alternatively, mindfulness also can be practiced by focusing internally and being aware of the flow and nature of your thoughts. This is a very powerful technique as it allows us to be observers of ourselves. There is a place from which we can stand back and observe the flow of our thoughts. Far too often we catch ourselves daydreaming or our brains feel "foggy". Learning to focus on tasks before us helps us to get them done faster and move to the next on the list.

Much more can be accomplished once we add mindfulness practices to meditation. It is related to our everyday tasks and emotional well-being, gaining knowledge and retaining it, thinking rationally, and having control over our emotions. While it may seem that meditation can help us to achieve these things, it is only because we have been misled to think that meditation includes the activities that bring us to being mindful.

Mindfulness is a form of concentration, focus or paying attention; mindfulness enables you to control your thoughts and change their direction or release them. Mindfulness also means being in the moment completely. It is not a method to relieve stress, but it can help to avoid it. When we encounter a stressful or even a scary situation, mindfulness helps the mind to quickly see outcomes from actions we might take. It helps us to notice details around us and keeps our thoughts on track rather than allowing ourselves to fall victim to the fight or flight reflex.

Meditation and Mindfulness Used Together

When used together, meditation and mindfulness help us in many ways. Meditation allows us to maintain inner awareness, balance and clarity in the midst of any situation, while mindfulness keeps us focused and grounded. It provides us with insight and clarity and may even help us come up with brilliant or even life-saving ideas at just the right moment. In the midst of normal daily life, mindfulness and meditation work together to help us to meet deadlines, remember the important details of a project, do well on exams or long written assignments, be better parents and have stronger relationships. They help us to say no to others when we are already too busy and can keep us happy and healthy. The benefits of meditation and mindfulness together are nearly endless.

Chapter 2

Common Misconceptions of Meditation

Many people have some common misconceptions about meditation. Some people believe that meditation is only done by yogis or gurus on top of a mountain in Tibet, during yoga, only done while lying down or sitting with your legs crossed, or it means going into a deep trance. In reality, meditation is safe and simple enough for everyone to practice and in no way does it cause danger- as long as you don't try to meditate while driving or in another serious situation that requires your attention.

- Meditation is just a relaxation technique – while it is an effective way to relax, there is more to meditation than just relaxation. Meditation teaches your body and mind how to relax quickly even in the face of danger so that your mind keeps working and stress does not overtake you.
- Meditation involves going into a trance – There is no need to go into a trance-like state to meditate. There are various techniques of meditation that range from

very simple exercises to help you to release your thoughts, to more complicated guided meditation journeys. It is up to each person to decide what is best for them.

- Meditation is a mysterious practice that cannot be understood– Again, meditation can be done by anyone at any age or station in life. It is not at all mysterious. It can be different for each person depending on what they chose to use it for, but a simple meditation technique can be beneficial even from the first time.
- It is dangerous and prudent people should avoid it – Meditation is extremely safe. It is in no way harmful to either the mind or the body. In fact, its' physical, mental, and emotional benefits can help people in many situations.
- Meditation is running from reality – The opposite is true because meditation helps people understand reality, gain self awareness, learn how to deal with stress calmly through reflection and allows us to make better decisions. It provides insight and clarity and enables you to see things as they truly are.

In short, meditation is very safe and easy to understand. Meditation is like mindfulness in that it helps us to be aware of our surroundings, our emotions, and ourselves. It helps us in many ways; physically, mentally, and emotionally to improve the quality of life for ourselves and those around us.

Chapter 3

A Thousand Year Old Practice

People around the world have practiced meditation for thousands of years. It has many names around the world but they are still the same concept. Meditation is an act of relaxation of the body and mind, it allows individuals to become mindful of their feelings and needs while also learning to be compassionate and understanding people. It helps us to "keep a good head on our shoulders", have a good heart, become more patient with others, and strive to live life in abundance and without stress.

The main focus of meditation, once people learn to relax and focus on their breathing is not to escape reality for a time or forget their worries, but to focus on their own internal being, the energy of their soul. A new age practitioner might call this something akin to talking to your Higher Self, which basically means that you communicate with your subconscious on levels that your cannot do with a cluttered mind. Meditation allows you to experience a gradual shift to a higher level of consciousness that is centered in peace, joy and awareness of your Soul.

If we take the time out of our busy lives to quietly communicate with ourselves and understand our own thoughts and desires, we can find solutions to our problems and answers to questions and anxieties that plague us. Some people question weather they are on the right career path or in the right relationship, while others want to activate their creative abilities and release their full potential. Yet others want to increase their vibration and move into a higher state of being. Whatever you find while meditating, it is what your subconscious wants you to know. Trust your intuition.

Mindfulness has only more recently been identified separately from meditation. In the past, the two had been bundled together. However, mindfulness is not a practice of communicating with your self-conscious or learning to relax the body and mind to reduce stress; it is an exercise of being in the moment at all times. Like meditation it helps to provide focus and an increased attention span, but it provides different benefits that are not necessarily attainable by meditation alone.

Although many people think of Eastern religion or New Age practitioners when they think of meditation, it is not a practice that requires following a religion or even a particular set of values. It is simply a tool used to make life better in many ways.

Chapter 4

The Power of Meditation

To many people it may seem that meditation is difficult at first, but the amazing thing about it is that even when not done perfectly it still offers many benefits and each time that it is done you become more accustomed to it. It becomes easier to slip into a relaxing rhythm of deep breathing and concentrating on that breath to get to a place of safe relaxation. It is so easy that literally anyone can do it by just following directions and gently allowing it to happen.

Advantages:
1. It is a method of deep relaxation and stress reduction
2. It requires no equipment and can be done alone
3. It can be done anywhere
4. No one ever has to know about it if you want it kept secret
5. Even beginners feel the benefits from the very first time

Anyone with anger issues, problems dealing with stress, insomnia, lack of focus, fears, or any problems in life can use meditation to conquer their problems. People with depression are sure to benefit by learning more about themselves and how to handle their emotions, as well as people with physical problems. No matter what the problem is that people face, meditation can help.

During meditation the mind and body are relaxed. It is as easy as resting your eyes and calming your thoughts for a quick break from the day. Our minds and bodies need these types of breaks from the constant stimulation we are bombarded with daily. We need time to stop processing information and emotions and just be. We need to be able to release the problems that cling to us long enough to deal with them.

It is impossible to completely rest the mind when the feelings, emotions, fears, and stress that drag us down are swimming in our heads. Meditation is a tool to relax the mind long enough and deeply enough to intentionally focus on those negativities using rationale and logic to examine them and how to deal with them. It helps you to find a new way of dealing with negativity and pessimism to make a conscious change in your life for the better. Even the most peaceful souls can benefit from meditation.

Mindfulness is a grounding technique and everyone should learn to be mindful in all moments of his or her life. Along with the benefits of meditation, mindfulness brings an ability to use the mind that becomes clear of negativity. Mindfulness allows people to function at higher levels, accomplish tasks more quickly without the stress of self-doubt. With a clear mind, the fog of uncertainty dissipates leaving focus, determination, and control over our actions.

Anyone who finds themselves replaying moments of their life over and over in their minds or is plagued by "what ifs" and hindsight can benefit greatly from mindfulness by learning to release thoughts that need to be addressed during a session of meditation at another time. Being in the moment- whether at work, at play, or at home, means that each moment can be fulfilling. We can choose our emotions, set them aside when we need to, and be a part of our own lives rather than just watching it go by.

Chapter 5

The Art of Meditation and Mindfulness

It can be easy to learn how to practice meditation and mindfulness, but the first step is to accept that it will help you and believe it will. Many times our minds block us from doing things because we are subject to our limiting beliefs, an example of one can be that it won't help or that others will think we are odd for practicing meditation. It is important to release any negative thoughts about the practice before your first session. If this is difficult, then it may be best to find someone to instruct you on steps to take to get into the right frame of mind.

Having an instructor can be helpful for anyone attempting meditation and mindfulness practices for the first time; some people prefer to have someone to follow their progress even for years. An instructor can make sure that you're comfortable, breathing correctly, and keep you focused on your goal even if you can't.

However, an instructor isn't necessary because these practices are simple enough for anyone who is truly ready to begin. After reading the explanations in this book, you can put them to use right away. The most important thing to remember is to be open to looking at your thoughts, emotions, and feelings as well as your reactions that come up, so that you can learn more about yourself and what you need to do to become a more confident, stronger, and happier person.

Before you Begin

Before you attempt meditation, there are some things that you may want to keep in mind. Making room for a new habit can be frustrating at first, but if something is important to you then you must find the time to do it. If you believe that it's important that you learn to understand your feelings, become more focused, gain invaluable insight and awareness and sleep more easily-then you must find the time to add meditation to your habits. Remember that forming habits takes time; don't become frustrated with yourself if you don't' meet your goals. Set aside the time and follow through on the promise you've made to yourself.

Try to choose a time of day when there are no outside pressures or time constraints, no one waiting for you, nothing to be done that will interfere with your peace. Your mind must be free of all of the hectic chaos so that you can settle down to a successful session. If there is anything that you feel must be done soon or you feel you might forget, write it down so that you can look at it later. This sends a signal to your mind that it's okay for you to forget those things for awhile. Put aside all of your negative thoughts and emotions as your begin so that you can feel as peaceful as possible.

It is also important to choose a place that provides peace and no distractions. Outdoors is a great place to meditate, but it must be free of things like biting insects and blinding sun. Early morning is a perfect time for this when the weather is nice; before the heat of day sets in and when the mind is perfectly clear. Practicing meditation outdoors provides fresh air and a connection to nature, which many of us lack in our technological world of computers and gadgets.

If you choose to meditate indoors, lighting a scented candle or incense can help to mask any smells that may be distracting, for instance, if someone is cooking. Soft music can block out sounds from other rooms. A focal point can help you to focus on one point and avoid wandering eyes if you prefer to keep your eyes open. All of these things can also help to set the habit of meditating daily by conditioning your mind and body to recognize certain sounds, sights and smells.

Goals for Beginners

When first starting out, you need to remember that there are goals to meet before you get started. These are very important in order to be as comfortable as possible and not be bothered by outside distractions:

Focus your attention – Being able to focus your attention internally is very important because you must be able to speak to your subconscious, connect with your Inner Self. It may take some time to connect and go deeper, but start out by remembering that the session is meant to help you to improve your life.

Deep, relaxed breathing – This is a part of the experience that helps you to bring plenty of oxygen into your body, feeding your brain and helping you to be focused. You must breathe deeply with long inhalations and exhalations. Not only does this raise your oxygen levels, but also helps you to focus on yourself. When you first start out, you may want to dedicate a few sessions to practicing breathing exercises to get used to the new activity before moving on.

Practice in quiet – Remove all distractions, or go to a place free of them. No animals, phones, loud clocks, television, radio, or anything else that might be distracting should be around. If noise seeping in from outside is a problem as it can be for people living in the city, purchase a relaxing recording of nature sounds or music that has no words. Calm, repetitive music can help to create the right ambience to help you focus. Listening with headphones on can be especially helpful when the distraction is quite loud.

Find a comfortable position – Many people begin in a seated position or lying down, but the most important things is comfort. This means that you must find a position that you can stay in without having your legs fall asleep or your clothing distracting you. Try to wear loose fitting or comfortable clothing when starting out.

How to Effectively Handle Distractions

It can be tough to avoid all of the distractions around us. Sounds, smells, sensations, even feelings can distract us from our goals in a meditative state. The first line of defense is meeting the goals previously described, however sometimes it is not possible to completely block out everything. If your dog starts barking, a car horn blares next door, or you just lose focus, there are ways to get back into the groove.

The single best way to get back into your meditation once distracted is to focus on your breathing. The deep steady breaths can easily be brought back under control, and with them you can bring your focus back into yourself. Just feel your breath coming in as your abdomen stretches, and feel it going out as it comes back in. Once the breathing is back under control, it should be relatively easy to get back into the session. Do not get frustrated with yourself if your thoughts wonder, it happens to everyone. Remember to remain non-judgmental and patient with yourself.

If the distraction is more than just a sound, for example a knock on the door from a delivery or neighbor, it is still beneficial to finish your allotted meditation time. Just get back into your comfortable position, concentrate on your focal point, music, or breathing, and complete your session. As you continue your practice it will become easier each time; if you find it frustrating just remind yourself all the reason why your practice is important to you.

Chapter 6
General Rules of Practice

Just as there are some basic goals, there are basic guidelines, or rules, that you may wish to follow. These are not meant to restrict your lifestyle, but to keep you comfortable and help you to avoid distraction.

Clothing

When first learning how to meditate, comfort is very important. You will want to choose clothing that is not too tight or that pinches. Try not to be too hot or too cold, wear what is appropriate to keep you as comfortable as possible so that there is as little distraction as possible. Comfort is the key.

Posture

Posture is important because you need to keep your spine straight to help your blood flow easily and to allow you to breathe deeply. Your position is much less important than keeping a straight spine. In any position you should be able to keep a good posture without straining or discomfort.

You may choose to sit in a recliner or simply lie down on your bed.

Don't be hungry, or full

A full stomach can take away from your brain function because blood is sent to the stomach and intestines as a part of the digestion process. If you are too full it can cause a distracting discomfort, but being hungry can cause this as well. If you are feeling hungry eat just enough to take away the hunger before attempting to meditate.

Don't come out of your session too fast

It is also important to remember not to jump right out of a session because it can be a bit of a shock to the system. Let your mind come back out into the world, let yourself hear the external sounds, and open your eyes slowly. Don't make any sudden movements or jump out of your position quickly. Take a few deep breathes and slowly start to move your fingers, hands and legs before getting up.

Chapter 7

Meditation Techniques and Exercises

For people who are new to meditation, it would be advisable to start out at home, indoors or outdoors, in a place that you feel safe and where you can control the distractions. With time and practice, the place or busyness of a quick session will not matter as much because it becomes very easy to do once you've tried it a few times.

In the beginning, you will likely find that you can only really focus and keep out distractions for five minutes here or ten minutes there, and that is expected. A good goal to keep in mind is 20 minutes of uninterrupted deep meditation. As you become accustomed to the practice, it becomes easier to add time until you have reached your goal. While setting out in the beginning, you can use a timer if you would like, or simply track your time with a stopwatch.

Attaining a State of Calm

A good beginning exercise in meditation is just to sit or lay very still and be aware of your thoughts, those that come and go, those that do not want to leave, and those that rise our emotions. Negative thoughts can be acknowledged in meditation without addressing them at the time. Thoughts that stick around may need to be addressed later, for example, guilt for being overweight, pain of a divorce, or anger over someone else's actions. Just let yourself *be* in this time, without judgment, guilt or jealously, pain or anger. Just be and see where your subconscious mind takes you while your conscious mind is occupied so that you can bring those problems out into the open and clear them out.

Relax the Body

Progressive muscle relaxation is an exercise where you totally relax and clear your mind, but this time focus on your body rather than your mind. Find your tension and acknowledge it, focusing on each tight place to help it to relax. Tell your body that it's okay to relax; that you're safe and that you don't need to do anything at all except just relax. It may be helpful to begin at the feet, working your way up your body, tightening areas and relaxing them completely as you go along. If you hold a lot of stress you may find that your upper body at the top of the back, shoulders, and neck resist relaxing the most. Concentrate on relaxing here last, but make sure that you become totally relaxed, even into your jaw, your tongue, and around your ears. This is the area where tension headaches oftentimes begin. This exercise can help to avoid or lessen them if you concentrate only on this area when stress comes up and you feel that you need to release it before a headache comes on.

Walking Meditation

Walking meditation requires a relaxation of the mind and awareness of the body together at once. Once you are able to easily slip into deep breathing and a relaxed state of mind, try it while walking, preferably in nature were there are no disturbances. Feel your body as it moves, the muscles as they flex and relax, the swinging motion of your arms, and the feel of your feet as they touch the ground. Keep your jaw relaxed and your tongue on the roof of your mouth behind your teeth. Feel the wind as it passes over your skin, the warmth of the sun. Keep your mind totally focused on your body and how it feels. If your mind wanders, bring it back to your breathing, your muscles and connect with your body while walking.

Some people also like to pay attention to nature during a walking meditation to reconnect with it and feel one with it. This could also be done in a seated position outdoors if preferred. If walking, your can spread your awareness out to the grass as it moves in the wind, butterflies, or flowers. If you feel drawn to something, go to it and let your awareness "feel" what has drawn you. See its details, take in its smell, and try to connect with it.

There are many other types of meditation, but these are some exercises for beginners looking for relaxation and relief from stress and the pressures of hectic lives. Once these become second nature or if you find yourself wanting more out of meditation, a little research will provide you with many other opportunities to expand your awareness.

Chapter 8

Mindfulness Techniques and Exercises

Mindfulness is more than just being in your mind and body during meditation. It means being aware in all moments, good, bad, even moments when you feel bored. Being mindful during meditation is part of the exercise in awareness of your thoughts and your body. It means that you are not allowing your mind to be completely empty or lost in space; you are still there even if your mind if free of thought, waiting for thoughts, and feelings to come along. You are feeling your tension areas and being 'mindful' that they are there.

Mindfulness in Times of Pain

You may be wondering how being mindful during times of pain can help us to be mindful in life. Life has many trials, and as we age or develop an illness like arthritis or Fibromyalgia we often try to distance or detach ourselves from that pain because it is uncomfortable. Many people with chronic pain complain of a foggy brain and an inability to concentrate; this can be attributed to the mind avoiding the pain felt by the body.

To learn to be mindful during times of pain, practice focusing on that pain during a meditation session. Go to the area of pain, maybe in a joint or a muscle, and feel that area. Go into the area closer and find the source of the pain, feel how it affects you and notice your emotional reaction. If the pain makes you want to shy away, be strong and stick with it. After a time the pain may shift a little, or even a lot. Go to that area and again concentrate on the source. Let your mind know that pain is just the body's way of letting us know that something is wrong or not working right. The most important point to remember is not to resist the pain, by accepting it and letting it flow through you will be able to release it.

In this exercise it may help to go back to a generalized area of pain or even back to the breath if needed. It can be difficult to concentrate on pain in the body just as it is hard to deal with painful memories. Over time, however, we can teach our minds that pain is just a part of the body and that it is okay to co-exist with it. There is no reason to hide from it. This strengthens our minds and gives us a sense of control over difficult times.

Mindfulness and Emotions

At times, emotions can run high and make us feel like we can do anything, while other times we feel depression, anger, fear, shame, or other emotions that stem from stray thoughts or experiences in our lives. During mediation, emotions can be used to allow us to observe our reactions internally, our reactions to others, and to see just how destructive they can be. If you are going through a hard time or have negative thoughts that come into your mind during meditation, you can spend some time examining the emotion, where it originates from and how it affects you. Without being judgmental, just make note of what happens to your body, your breath, and how it changes.

When you feel depressed, angry, or guilty, think about the root cause of these emotions. How does it make your body feel, and where is it centered in your body? What makes it intensify or ease up? How is it affecting your moods or decisions? Try looking at it all as only an observer without feeling the emotions in a way that is very disturbing to your experience. With this method you may discover things about yourself that open your eyes and give you insight as to why you may have certain destructive behaviors or little motivation. Over time, it can become easier to look at emotions as they come up, analyze them quickly, decide that they are not worth the effort and let them go.

Mindfulness and Wandering Thoughts

Sometimes when we are mindful of our stray thoughts we find self-doubt or judgment of our actions and ourselves. We might find that we believe deep down that we are not able to do things that we consciously know we can actually do. We might shy away from relationships because we fear rejection or not bother to dress nice or look nice to others because we subconsciously have little confidence. Of the many possibilities, these are ones that hold us back from making advancements in our lives.

Set aside some time during meditation to look at stray thoughts and examine how they make you feel. Are they tied to something dark in your past? Can you determine how they make your body feel? If you tense up from a thought, where is the tension? If you find that stray thoughts are tied to something in your past, like an unhealthy relationship or a bully, can you somehow break that tie? Try to look at thoughts or memories that cause interference logically. Ask yourself if there is something that you can change about them, or another experience that you can tie them to, see if that helps over time.

In our daily lives, stray thoughts come up and sometimes take us for a ride. We can learn to be mindful and put them away for later. We can chose to stay in our current moment rather than daydream about the future or revisit past experiences.

Chapter 9

Meditation Exercises For Raising Vibrations

Do you ever feel like you're not worthy to achieve financial abundance and will never amount to anything? That you are too old or that you failed too many times? Is perhaps guilt holding you back from achieving your goals because you believe you're not worthy to feel joyful and happy? Whatever comes to mind is your limiting belief and the reason why you've struggled; you can shatter that by reprogramming your subconscious mind. It may not always be obvious exactly what those reasons are. However, by practicing mindfulness and meditation you will be able to gain deep insight and awareness into your subconscious self-image of yourself. You will never earn more income or lose more weight then what your hidden self-image will allow you to. If you have a dream but have a counter-intention (limiting belief about this) hidden in your mind, you will never achieve that dream. This means that your logical and emotional brains have to sync up, that is your subconscious and conscious minds. Your self-image and self-worth is how you feel about yourself internally. If you want to start changing your self-image the first step is acceptance.

The first step is to unconditionally accept where you are, right now, right here in this moment. No matter if you are out on the street or are forty pounds overweight. Accept it. This alone will lower your anxiety because as long as you are worried about the future, you are without power. You are putting all your energy into what "could be, should be". You may feel intense and shut yourself down, your brain will not work effectively and you won't be able to help yourself. Most people don't realize that acceptance is a proactive state. It will move you forward, your brain will actually grow new pathways and you will start to be the most effective you've ever been. This does not mean you have to be okay with what the current results or circumstances but it does take the pressure off of you. It does not mean you are giving in. The power within you gets activated and as soon as you click into acceptance mode everything opens up.

Exercise For Clearing Blocks and Accepting the Present

Accepting where you are, in this moment, time and place can be a door opener and a catalyst for change. By unconditionally accepting where you are and being in a complete state of awareness can be a life changing experience, as acceptance is a proactive state. Acceptance does not mean that you are being passive and are not doing anything about it. This is very important to understand. Acceptance gets you to a place from where you can move on.

- Start out in a very comfortable position with lights dim or your favorite scented candle burning. Close your eyes and take a few deep breaths and accept your breathing, just as you would accept the stars in the sky.

- The moment you do, your breathing relaxes- do this exercise with any trauma, abuse, anger etc. The next step is to SURRENDER wherever you are emotionally, physically or spiritually and accept this.
- Let thoughts arise and do not judge them. As long as you are judging yourself and feeling frustrated, you are blocking yourself. The key is to stop feeling frustrated and to stop resisting unwanted feelings and allow them to pass through you. Ask for more of it and you'll see that the uncomfortable feeling dissipates. The more frequently you do this and practice, the faster you will be able to let things go that do not serve you.

Exercise For Letting Go of the Past

People often hold on to and can't let go of failures, regrets, family and relationship issues. These are things that block us and use up a lot of energy as we think and ruminate day in and day out.

Another powerful exercise to help us 'Let Go' is to once again accept your breathing and focus on exhales. Hold in your mind the issue or problem and while exhaling say your own name to yourself. Do this continuously for five minutes. This is a very powerful technique for letting go. You may choose to do this outside or inside while doing something you love such as gardening or playing the piano. By accepting and letting go you are allowing the 'golden seeds to grow' making room for a new vision. The biggest mistake people make is that they underestimate themselves.

Change can happen instantaneously; whatever has happened in the past- let it go so that it doesn't take any more of your brain's power. Only then you can focus on other things and move forward. If you do not know what is holding you back, the best thing you can do is give it a voice, accept it and let it go. The answer will come to you, oftentimes during meditation.

Exercise for Overcoming Unpleasant Emotions

Don't judge your emotions. This means you drop the 'negative and bad' from your vocabulary. Instead they are just "unpleasant". Feelings are tied to bodily sensations. The thing you are trying to shy away from is the thing that let's you know what you are feeling. We back away because we don't want to experience unpleasant sensations ie. shame-avoidance, pain-avoidance or guilt-avoidance. We need to be able to understand that feelings are connected to our bodies and come in waves. Usually this lasts around 90 seconds and varies in intensity but it will not last longer than that. When we think about the same thing we keep firing the same sequence in our brain.
People maintain the belief that their prior life story is true to maintain consistency and not get out of their comfort zone. What you need to do is expand your window of tolerance. One of the great ways of overcoming this is through affirming to yourself "I am open and willing to experience things that will cause me discomfort and/or be uncomfortable". This facilitates change and gets you out of

the comfort zone. Through practice you can reduce the unpleasantness.

Make a pre-commitment to yourself. Say to yourself, "when I feel this emotion, I pre-commit to ride the wave", you will then be able to get through that emotion and each time the feeling will last a shorter amount of time. Stay well connected to your body. If something feels unpleasant, do it ANYWAYS. If you do it repetitively enough, you will achieve a new comfort level. You will start to see yourself as resourceful and capable.
Acquiring the right mindset is only one piece of the puzzle. The second skill you need to acquire is your tolerance for risk needs to be higher. Only by mastering your emotions you can get to the next level. Mindfulness and mediation techniques will help you achieve this.

Steps to take to overcome your emotional past:

1. Recognize what is holding you back.
2. Accept it.
3. Make a commitment to yourself to release it.
4. Reprogram your brain by 'riding the wave' and 'fake it until you make it'.

Remember, things that happened in the past have nothing to do with the future. What happened in the past is irrelevant to what is happening right now. Commit yourself to let go of things that no longer serve you.

Chapter 10

Attracting Abundance Through Mindfulness

Practicing mindfulness is absolutely essential to creating abundance. The first thing you have to realize is that by being in a state of love, peace and gratitude is to be in the super vibrational level. From this level attracting the things you want is effortless. However, when you are in a state of fear, for example thinking about debt- you can instantly feel your body tense and you start to get anxious. It is important to recognize that anytime you're not feeling good- you are causing those feelings to occur and not the external environment. You are telling yourself a story about the external environment. It's your thought about what's going on and this is what is causing you to feel a certain way. Always look for the silver lining and practice re-framing. This can be a very powerful tool.

You must be able to uncover your hidden and unconscious beliefs because until you do your unconscious mind will govern your physical world. No matter how great your intentions are, whatever manifests in your physical word is directly aligned with what your subconscious believes. If you are not sure of what you have programmed in your subconscious, look at your life. Your entire life is a blueprint of your subconscious mind. Whatever you think is good that comes into your life, it does so because you have programs to support that coming in. Anything that you have to work very hard at, anything you struggle with, anything you have to put effort into is because you have programs that allow this to happen. It is important to pinpoint these negative traits and identify them because they will keep on sabotaging you. You want to break those sabotaging patterns and get over your habitual ways of thinking and behaving. Look at areas of your life that are not working. Look at the results you have achieved. Choose an area for example your finances or relationship and ask yourself: what thoughts and beliefs do I have around this? This will help you to identify any negative thoughts and/or limiting beliefs you may have about this subject.

You must reprogram both the conscious and subconscious minds and two of the most powerful ways of doing that are through mindfulness and meditation. Mindfulness is especially useful. One example is by using positive affirmations. By affirming to yourself that "all is well" and 'abundance is my birthright" daily, enables you to reprogram your conscious mind. Daily affirmations can encourage a positive attitude and a strengthening of resolve. Meditation allows you to retrain the subconscious mind by reprogramming it and substituting limiting beliefs with healthy beliefs. This way The Law of Attraction matches your subconscious beliefs. And this is why it's so important to get clear of the counter-intentions your subconscious mind holds.

You must come to an understanding that you are a spiritual being living temporarily in a physical body. From this you build and realize that you are where you are because of all thoughts, feelings and beliefs you have about yourself. You must shift your awareness from who you think you are (physical body) to who you really are- a spiritual being having a human experience. You must think of yourself as infinite, you are a piece of GOD or the Universe. It's difficult to buy into this concept because we have been convinced through the conditioning process that we are what the senses tell us. Changing habits is something many people have difficultly with but you can start by reprogramming your subconscious mind.

The first thing you must do to attract abundance is to imagine how you'd like your life to look like. In order to change anything in your life you have to change the concept of yourself. The concept of yourself is everything you believe about yourself to be true. This concept has landed you wherever you are right now in your life and is the result of your subconscious mind. Whatever is working, whatever is not working, any illness you may be suffering form; even if you struggle with weight is related to what you have come to believe about yourself. In order to change any of those things you must be able to change what you have come to believe as true. These are the things that have been imposed on us in our childhood, society and culture in which we were raised.

All this programming has been downloaded into our subconscious just like computer software and is now running on autopilot. Mindfulness will enable you to pay attention to all the habits you have acquired and all the thoughts that are part of you. Live in the feeling of what you want your dream to be and your dream will be realized. Pay attention to your soul- notice where you are weak, where you are incapable and realize that these are areas presented to you as ones you have to work on because the true essence of your soul is that it wants to grow and expand. It does not want to be restricted; the part of you that has prevented you from growth is the part that tells you how depressed, sad, weak or anxious you are. Begin to pay attention to your soul; all it wants is to grow.

In order to manifest your dreams or wishes, you have to get yourself to a place where you expect it of yourself and then you must be able to visualize it. If you can't imagine it, it can't manifest into physical reality and won't be possible. You must evoke a feeling that your dream has already been fulfilled, that it's happening. This is a very difficult thing for people to do and is more than just an intellectual exercise. Even though you may have all sorts of resistance come up from past experience and your senses may even tell you it's impossible; even when everyone you run into tells you it can't be done, you must be able to feel as if you already have it- even though it has not shown up in your physical reality yet.

This is what oftentimes people mean by the phrase "fake it until you make it". Treat yourself as it was already in your existence. By doing this you are demonstrating a great deal of faith and for this alone you will be rewarded. Develop the will power to change your thoughts. Once you are aware you have choice, your greatest power is your ability to accept or reject information. Think only the highest thoughts that support your purpose. Everything else- let it go.

THE MOST EFFECTIVE WAYS TO INCREASE VIBRATION and MANIFEST ABUNDANCE:

- Choose your circle of friends carefully. Positivity is contagious. Do not hang around people who bring you down to the victim level. As the saying goes: If you want to fly like an Eagle don't surround yourself by a bunch of turkeys!
- Unleash the past, forgive yourself and others and accept the present. Don't let negativity from the past chain you down.
- Be grateful for everything in your life. Feeling gratitude is the #1 way to increase your vibration and bring about abundance. It will allow you to move forward.
- Laugh as much as you can. Laughter is great for the soul.
- Smile more often. Just by smiling you are changing your energy pattern.
- Turn off the news. Daily news is filled with negativity and is bound to bring you down. **7.** Unless you can watch it without getting emotionally charged- omit it altogether.
- Read success and spiritual literature. Brainwash yourself in abundance. Keep feeding your mind.
- Re-frame your thoughts to Up-Thinking. This means that instead of thinking "what is the worst that can happen" think to yourself "what if something wonderful happens" expect miracles- magic and miracles occur all the time. Allow the universe to delight and surprise you.

- Take 100% responsibility for what happens to you in life. Remember, you are 100% responsible for what shows up.
- Practice meditation and mindfulness daily. Meditation brings about clarity, joy, peace, and tranquility. Meditation also creates an opening in your life to receive inspiration.
- Take inspired action and be clear about what you want. Begin by taking the smallest step (the one you can take today).
- Affirm to yourself daily: ABUNDANCE IS MY BIRTHRIGHT. ALL IS WELL.

Conclusion

By now it should be easy to see that mindfulness can be a part of meditation, but it is actually a practice in itself. Meditation is often used to relax the mind and body, provide a respite from stress and bridge awareness between the mind and body. It helps us to clear out negative thoughts so we can think clearly and focus. Meditation has many benefits but among others it lowers high blood pressure, helps us to fall asleep easier, and we gain valuable insight and awareness about ourselves along the way.

Mindfulness keeps us in the moment, always grounded and present in the body. It is not a clear state of mind as meditation often is. Being mindful helps us deal with pain and pressures as they occur, and even learn to release negative feelings immediately if we decide they are not serving us. As children, bullies can hurt our feelings and make us feel bad about ourselves, but sometimes as adults we can just ignore words of mean people because they don't matter to us. If we don't deal with those painful moments in life right away they get stored in the subconscious and become stray thoughts or suppressed feelings about ourselves that need to be addressed to allow us to be our best in life. Meditation exercises for letting go of the past can help us clear many blocks and achieve a higher state of vibration from which we can attract abundance into our life.

Working with meditation and mindfulness together brings peace into our lives, a peace that most people will never experience. Not only is it a safe practice, but also a healthy one that makes us happier, more compassionate people, understanding of others and ourselves. We learn to focus our energies in the right direction at the right times to accomplish more. Meditation is a tool that helps us gain awareness as well peace and tranquility to be the people that we want to be; it allows us to let go of our fears, insecurities and emotions that hold us back from achieving our full potential. Mindfulness and meditation create openings in your life to receive inspiration. Learn to follow inspiration and trust it. Remember, there is no such thing as a "failure". There is only a result that you learn from...

Sending you lots of light and love,
Ingrid

Made in the USA
Columbia, SC
10 March 2022